How Big Is Our Baby?

wren
&rook

First published in Great Britain in 2019 by Wren & Rook
This edition published in Great Britain in 2019 by Wren & Rook

Text copyright © Smriti Prasadam-Halls, 2019
Illustration copyright © Britta Teckentrup, 2019

ISBN: 978 1 5263 6040 3
E-book ISBN: 978 1 5263 6060 1
10 9 8 7 6 5 4 3 2 1

Wren & Rook
An imprint of
Hachette Children's Group
Part of Hodder & Stoughton
Carmelite House
50 Victoria Embankment
London EC4Y 0DZ

An Hachette UK Company
www.hachette.co.uk
www.hachettechildrens.co.uk

Publishing Director: Debbie Foy
Senior Editor: Liza Miller
Art Director: Laura Hambleton
Designer: Sally Griffin

Printed in China

For bouncy new babies
and the big brothers and sisters
who love them – S.P–H.

For Irina – B.T.

smriti prasadam-halls • britta teckentrup

How Big Is Our Baby?

Congratulations!

You're going to have a baby **brother** or **sister**.

That means you're going to be a **big** brother or sister soon!

This little person will be a brand-new friend to play with. You're going to be a **very** important part of their life.

After all, they're going to need someone to teach them lots of clever things as they grow up … and that's **you**!

After hearing such big news, you're bound to have lots of feelings.

Happy!

Curious!

Impatient!

It's **wonderful** news,
so make sure you celebrate.

You may also feel a little worried. Soon you're going to be sharing your family, your toys and your home with a new someone.

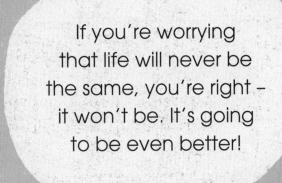

If you're worrying that life will never be the same, you're right – it won't be. It's going to be even better!

There's going to be **MORE** fun, **MORE** cuddles and **MORE** love.

Everything needs time and a safe place to grow.

After all,
flowers grow
in rich soil.

And cupcakes
rise in a warm
oven.

A baby is just the same. It needs to live somewhere safe and warm while it develops and gets strong. That's a special place inside your mum called the **womb**.

Pregnancy is the name we give to the nine months that the baby spends in the womb. There, the baby is fed and protected as it gets bigger and bigger, until it is ready to come out and meet you.

Let's explore how Baby is going to develop during pregnancy!

1

month

Baby is as small as a speck of **sand** at the seaside.

Baby is **tiny**!

A special code for Baby is already in place. It's like a unique **recipe** that comes from both parents, and controls things like hair colour, eye colour and skin tone.

Soon this little someone will have **eyes**, **ears**, a **nose** and a **mouth**.

What colour are your eyes?

2

months

Baby is the size of a **jelly bean**.

Baby may still be small, but the most important parts of its body are in place. The **heart** pumps blood, the **brain** thinks and the **lungs** will help Baby breathe.

Our little one has a heartbeat! It's too gentle to feel at the moment, though.

Believe it or not, Baby has a tiny **tail** and **webbed feet**. Don't worry, they'll disappear soon.

Put your hand over your heart and see if you can feel your own heartbeat. It helps if you do five star jumps first!

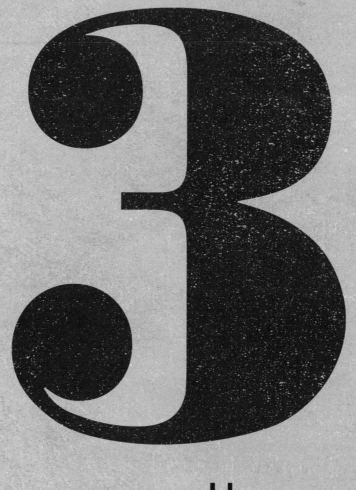

3
months

Baby is the size of an **egg**.

While growing in the womb,
Baby is known as a **foetus**.

The tiny tot has **fingers**
and **toes**, just like you.

**How many
fingers and toes
do you have?**

Baby gets at least twice as heavy
during this month. Just imagine if you
doubled your weight in four weeks!

4 months

Baby is the size of a **pear**.

This month, you may be able to discover if Baby is a **boy** or a **girl**. Some families like to find out, and others prefer to have a surprise when Baby is born.

The little one is growing **eyebrows** and **hair**.

Baby can start making finger movements.

Wriggle your fingers and wave to Baby!

5 months

Baby is the size of a **mango**.

Baby can hear **sounds** now.

Sing a song so the little one can get to know your voice!

Baby is wiggling and jiggling all around.

Your mum might feel Baby **move** for the very first time. It's a fluttery feeling in the womb – imagine if a butterfly was inside your tummy!

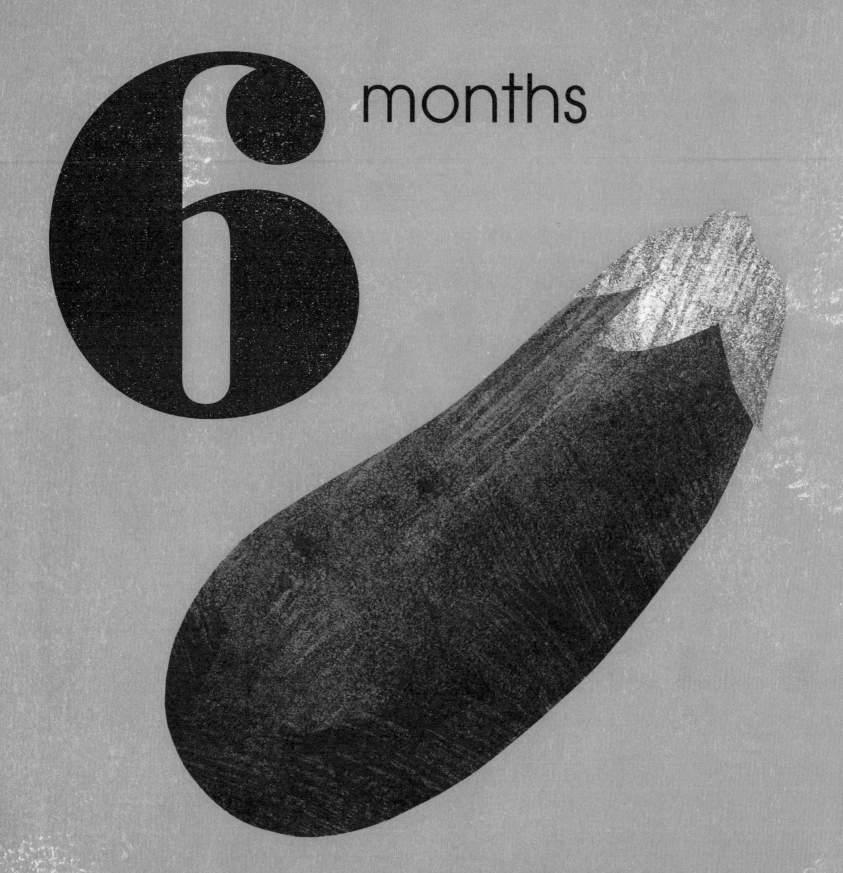

6 months

Baby is the size of an **aubergine**.

Baby can **smile** and make **funny faces**.

Baby's **brain** is growing all the time. Tell the little one about something you've learnt today.

Have you thought of any names for Baby?

7 months

Baby is the size of a **cauliflower**.

Baby might be doing some really big **kicks**.

Ask if you can feel them. Perhaps Baby is going to be a footballer or a dancer!

Baby is getting bigger and stronger from the good food your mum is eating. A special **cord** passes food between her and the little one.

Baby is also growing little **eyelashes**.

8 months

Baby is the size of a **football**.

Baby is now probably upside down in your mum's womb, getting into position to be born. Can you imagine being on your head all day?

Baby can sleep and dream, just like you!

Baby sleeps and wakes at different times each day and night.

What do you think Baby is doing right now?

9 months

Baby is the size of a **watermelon**.

Baby is so **big**. Imagine carrying a heavy watermelon around with you all day! Can you think of some ways to help your mum when she's feeling tired?

The little one can **blink**, **cry**, **sleep** and **smile** … even **suck** their **thumb**.

Thumbs up little Baby, you're ready to be born!

When Baby comes

Usually Baby decides when to arrive, but sometimes the **birth** of a baby is planned for a particular day.

Some babies are born in **hospital** and some are born at **home**.

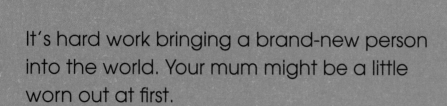

It's hard work bringing a brand-new person into the world. Your mum might be a little worn out at first.

She will need lots of rest!

Wherever and whenever Baby arrives, he or she is going
to be **excited** to meet you. Be ready to give Baby
a lovely, big, warm **welcome** into your family!

To begin with, it may seem like Baby does a great deal of **sleeping**, **crying** and **feeding**! But it's all really important if Baby is going to grow into a healthy, strong person. Your parents might not be able to play as much as usual while they're looking after the little one – but that doesn't mean they don't want to play at all.

Why don't you bring some books to them while they're feeding Baby, or show everyone some of your drawings?

Some of the things you do every day may change a little. But there's one thing you can be sure won't change – you'll still be **loved** as much as ever.

You may have lots of good ideas about how to help with Baby. Your family will love to hear your suggestions – just make sure to ask first before you do anything.

Baby will love it if you **talk, sing songs** and pull **funny faces**. Babies love to laugh!

Don't forget to add in plenty of cuddles and kisses.

Your most important job is to enjoy getting to know Baby. Because this beautiful, bouncy baby isn't just **any** baby …

... it's your VERY OWN baby brother or sister!

NIGHT VISION

NIGHT VISION

The Art of Urban Exploration by Troy Paiva foreword by Geoff Manaugh

CHRONICLE BOOKS
SAN FRANCISCO

For Mom, who gave me the ability to see. For Dad, who gave me the love of machines.

Library of Congress Cataloging-in-Publication Data
available.

ISBN: 978-0-8118-6338-4

Manufactured in China
Designed by Matthew Boyd and River Jukes-Hudson

10 9 8 7 6 5 4 3 2 1

Chronicle Books LLC
680 Second Street
San Francisco, California 94107

www.chroniclebooks.com

CONTENTS

In his now classic book *The Rings of Saturn*, author W. G. Sebald visits an abandoned military base on England's East Anglian coast. The "closer I came to these ruins," he writes, "the more I imagined myself amidst the remains of our own civilization after its extinction in some future catastrophe." Sebald suggests that the derelict concrete structures left scattered here and there in the diffuse maritime light "resembled temples or pagodas," even tombs, or "the tumuli in which the mighty and powerful were buried in prehistoric times with all their tools and utensils, silver and gold."

Hiking through those coastal ruins alone, consumed by his own particular brand of awed Romanticism, Sebald even seems unsure the site had been constructed by humans at all. He soon becomes filled with the pervasive and unshakable sense that he is actually standing "on ground intended for purposes transcending the profane." Indeed, "wandering about among heaps of scrap metal and defunct machinery, the beings who had once lived and worked here were an enigma." What strange race would leave such spaces behind? Transformed now by time, weather, and the absence of basic maintenance, what were once buildings had become abstract mounds, suggestions of shapes, tumid outgrowths dotting the horizon—not architecture at all, then, but something more strange and inexplicable: structural blurs without identifiable purpose or history.

Such is the often unacknowledged appeal of destruction. Even the most familiar scenes, given time and allowed to collapse under their own weight, colonized by birds, rats, and vegetation, will become literally uncanny, somehow foreign to the very culture that constructed them.

Ruins have always had a certain emotional or artistic appeal; this is as true for wrecked airplanes as it is for Gothic cathedrals. We no longer need to visit the fallen domes and rain-stained masonry of churches in rural Europe, or even the old stone temples of Angkor Wat, to see ever-widening cracks in the façade of human settlement. We simply have to drive to the other side of town or walk past boarded-up storefronts after dusk.

We are surrounded by ruins—it's just a question of noticing them.

In Troy Paiva's work we see the wrecked urban edges and unpopulated landscapes of the American West. The 20th century, as his photographs show, produced its own spectacular, seemingly posthuman ruins. In

DESERT ILIAD   Geoff Manaugh

6

the cities, deserts, and hills of California, extending out to the bleached margins of the state and into Nevada, Arizona, and Utah, passing east along arterial highways into Texas, we have inherited a semi-toxic world of old military equipment and abandoned shopping malls—wastefully complex and tinged with melancholy, but gorgeous nonetheless.

Paiva's images of airplane graveyards, in particular, are all the more evocative and gripping when you consider that his father was a flight engineer, hopping planes from country to country. In his book *The Atrocity Exhibition*, J. G. Ballard describes a surreal landscape of crashed bombers, abandoned air warfare ranges, and disused runways. He refers to such images as "the nightmare of a grounded pilot," or "the suburbs of Hell," a "University of Death," across which people wander, stunned by the ruins all around them.

It seems obvious to point out here that if the Romantics, for instance, had written their poems in a different geographic or historical context— if they had grown up in detached houses on cul-de-sacs at the sprawling outer rim of California's desert suburbia, in Palmdale, or outside Bakersfield—then they may not have planned their famously poetic trips to see the picturesque remains of shattered abbeys lost in mist. But the quasi-archaeological eyes of those poets and artists would still be enraptured today. Wordsworth could very well have gone out at 2 AM on a weeknight to see the cracked windshields of car wrecks on the sides of desert roads, new ruins from a different and arguably more interesting phase of Western civilization. Or perhaps someone like Caspar David Friedrich would, even now, be climbing through the shells of abandoned hotels, stopping to snap a few pictures beneath the weathered plywood screens of drive-in cinemas, exploring those archaeologies so particular to our own point in history. Instead of tours through Classical ruins on the outskirts of Athens and Rome, they would be urban explorers of concrete blocks and two-by-fours, following train tracks through the dirt.

After all, we live in an unexpected golden age for dereliction. Today's accelerated rate of replacement just means we have more and more things to leave behind—and this ever-growing trail of wreckage, Paiva's work shows, leads full circle and around again, back to the very heart of the American dream. This book documents the architectural discard pile of a whole nation, an orphaned version of ourselves that we no longer want or need, some long-lost twin of the present moment cut adrift to wander alone in the empty.

Hike far enough and you'll find yesterday; it's sitting at the end of the street or on the other side of that mountain range—and tomorrow is right next to it. Time is a landscape.

People may go into the desert to rid themselves of things—to be rid of themselves, perhaps—but what they thought they'd left behind now resides out there, unclaimed, camouflaged rather than truly surrendered. You throw something away on the road out of town and it *remains* there, unintentionally exhibited for the next generation, and the next, and the next. Even cigarette butts become evidence for a future archaeology, the whole landscape now a museum of forgotten objects, temporarily covered then revealed again by shifting sand—and all of it is so dark we must cast our own lights so that we can illuminate these traces more fully.

Among other things, Paiva's photographs show that even decay can last, ironically, becoming monumental in its own right. That specific gas station or factory, those particular rooms and warehouses, may even disappear just days after he has visited them—but the process of decay remains, that slow destruction settled there like a virus inside the landscape, structurally active behind the surface of new frontages and fresh paint. Decay, strangely, gives the past a new, unearthly future, signs of an older world transformed.

Paiva shows us what historical dead ends actually look like: cities reduced to shells, their buildings empty, a planet devoid of inhabitants. Yet, for all its melancholy, this book is meditative. We stare at the abandoned cranes, barns, and villages, the rusting infrastructures of a civilization whose sole purpose now is to waste away, eroding down to another stage of itself. It is a *military / industrial sublime*. And there is calm in that—an inevitability, a mythology we might even find ourselves looking forward to.

CONFESSIONS OF AN URBAN EXPLORER   Troy Paiva

"Urban exploration," a term coined in 1996 by Jeff "Ninjalicious" Chapman in his zine *Infiltration,* is the investigation of the man-made places ignored and largely unseen by the public. Most are either abandoned military / industrial installations or operating infrastructural sites. All of these locations are generally off-limits, requiring either stealthy, sometimes risky, trespassing, or permission from owners and caretakers to gain access. Given the relentless drive of humans to both build and explore, it's safe to say that urban exploration is a pastime as old as mankind. It's simply how we're wired.

As with the Sierra Club, the urban exploration (frequently shortened to UrbEx or UE) mantra is "Take only pictures and leave only footprints." For both groups, the idea is to glide through the scene, absorbing the atmosphere and stillness. But that's where the similarities end—UrbEx sites bear no resemblance to a serene mountain glen. This is a world of beautiful decay and sexy squalor, oozing with a sense of transience and loss. You can feel the echoes of former human habitation—not "ghosts" in a cornball movie sense, but ghosts nonetheless.

UrbEx means different things to different people. For some, it's about infiltrating a city's storm drains and subway tunnels. For others, it's climbing bridges and radio towers. Generally speaking, though, UrbEx is the exploration of TOADS (Temporary, Obsolete, Abandoned, and Derelict Spaces). Industrial complexes, military installations, junkyards, asylums, hotels—you name it. Since the '70s, my main area of interest has been the deserts of the American Southwest, concentrating on 20th-century roadside ghost towns, but my scope has expanded in the last ten years to include just about any lapsed spaces. For most explorers, if it's derelict and run-down, it's fair game.

There are many schools of thought on what kinds of sites are the best. The TOADS explored often simply depend on what's available nearby to explorers. The Northeast is home to the Rust Belt's abandoned industry, as well as legendary old hospitals and asylums. In the West you'll find decommissioned military bases and some of the best junkyards and abandoned roadsides in the world. Wherever the location, the urban explorer's soul remains the same: We're all in search of our own entropical paradise.

Pop culture offers a glimpse of the UrbEx experience. The film industry often makes use of the atmosphere in UrbEx-style locations as a modern industrial analog to the castles and forests from older literature: consider

Sodium Clouds, 2007 (opposite). The pump island at the forgotten "Lockhart Ranch" general store and gas station in Lockhart, California. Seventy-five miles away, the Los Angeles metroplex lights up the clouds.

the chase through the sewers of Vienna in *The Third Man*, or the dank moldy school where the characters are holed up and the tunnel through which they escape in *Children of Men*, or the final shootout in the abandoned factory in *The French Connection*. Hundreds of examples exist in every other medium, from comic books to opera. A sense of forboding—that something important is about to happen in these creepy places—has been instilled in us for generations by our entertainment. This may be part of why most people are intimidated and frightened by these kinds of places. Whenever they see them, the hero is in danger. But it also explains the appeal for urban explorers: these spaces are the settings for adventures, and at times, come with real risk.

Many of us first began exploring abandoned places as part of a childhood rite of passage anthropologists and folklorists have dubbed "Legend Tripping"—that "I double-dog-dare you to go in that spooky old house!" experience. Yet I never lost the desire to check out places that were off-limits—the older I got, the more obsessed I became. The intoxicating rush of entering forbidden territory, coupled with the brooding silence of these places, drew me in and never let go.

In over twenty-five years of urban exploring, I've seen hundreds of locations disappear: ripped apart by vandals, burned down, bulldozed, subdivided—sometimes even blown up by film crews. As of this writing, many of the locations and machines in this book are already gone.

That knowledge is part of what makes UrbEx such an evocative pursuit: the realization that explorers only have a short time with these places—the feeling that they've reached the ends of their lifetimes is ever present. It's easy to become passionate about a place, but it's best to temper it with the understanding that the relationship will be short and poignant. Each visit may be your last. Yes, it's natural to be sad and disappointed when a site is gone, but you have to let it go, with the understanding that this is the cycle for *everything*.

For instance, there's a part of me that wants the soon to be renovated Oakland train station (pages 60–74) to remain neglected and decrepit, a dark and somber monument to failed technology. At the same time, part of me is glad it's being saved. Maybe in a hundred years it will be derelict again, awaiting rediscovery by a future urban explorer.

This is just how I approach the idea of urban exploration. The first thing on most people's minds when encountering these abandoned places is "Who is going to clean this up?" or "Can the money be raised to restore this to its former glory?"—but not me. I don't explore to become involved with preservation battles or to ponder the political and ethical implications of these places. I accept that this is the natural process of things, the logical progression of life and death. Where most see waste and blight, I see elegant devolution and the weight of time. The idea of billions of dollars' worth of taxpayer money lying abandoned in desolate, toxic military ruins doesn't make me frustrated or angry; it makes me want to take pictures. I revere and honor the *wabi-sabi* soul of these places by recording their decline, an impartial observer recording the final moments of a crumbling man-made world that few ever get to see.

I began exploring as a teenager in the 1970s, driving the American deserts looking for derelict places and machines. In those days it was called "ghost towning," even though it had more to do with the run-down 20th-century roadside than the Wild West.

By the end of the '80s, I had discovered night photography and immediately connected it to the abandoned places I explored. After seeing the lighting work of photographers O. Winston Link, William Lesch, and Chip Simons, my head exploded with the creative potential of combining light painting with moonlit time exposures. Thinking of these desolate locations as dark stage sets, I experimented with controlling the mood and atmosphere using color, intensity, and chiaroscuro, always in the pursuit of heightening the otherworldly nature of the settings. I continued to wander the West, only now in the middle of the night, with a funky old Canon FX 35mm camera, bought at a swap meet for forty bucks. It felt artistically purer for me to be taking these surreal pictures of junk *with* junk. Over the course of ten years, I built a body of work that eventually became the LostAmerica.com Web site in 1998 and the book *Lost America* in 2003. By 2004, however, the road trips were taking their toll, and I was constantly aggravated by the low yield of usable work from my ancient equipment. As the film era fizzled out, I was further stymied by lab closures and sloppy processing. Frustrated, I stopped shooting for almost a year.

At about this time, affordable digital camera technology had reached the point where noise-free, minutes-long exposures were possible. Seeing buttery-smooth digital night work for the first time shocked me into the realization that the future was here—now. So I bought a Canon 20D

11

digital SLR camera and began experimenting with the exposure and lighting techniques I had developed throughout the '90s.

As I was easing my way back into night photography, some local urban explorers who knew my previous work contacted me about going shooting with them. This was an indication of how the cult of UrbEx had grown; just ten years prior I would have been hard-pressed to find people to shoot with. As with many obscure pursuits, the Internet pulled the culture closer together. Until this point, my urban exploring and night photography had been a solitary pursuit, but I felt that shooting with others was part of the change that came with picking up a camera again. Plus, they knew some killer locations! Before I even realized it, the bug had bit me again. Fueled by the new ability to huddle around the digital camera-preview grunting "ooh, ooh, ooh!" (a.k.a. "chimping the shot"), the instant gratification of posting work online, and the timely ripening of some craptacular locations, I began shooting at a shocking rate. In two years I captured more images in more new locations than I had in the previous ten. Most of this book is culled from that work.

All of these images were shot at night. A few were done in the last moments of dusk, but most were taken in full darkness. The work from before 2005 was done on film; all the rest was shot digitally. The exposure times run from a few seconds to eight minutes, with most in the two- to four-minute range. All the images were also taken within a few nights of the full moon, and for the exteriors the moon was the primary light source. The light painting was done during the exposure with a strobe flash and a wide variety of flashlights. I use swatches of theatrical lighting gels to add color to the light. I don't use light stands or compli- cated rigging—all my lighting is handheld. Observers are often surprised by my low-tech techniques, asking "Is that all there is to it?" I have to keep it simple because this is frequently a guerrilla style of photography. Traveling light is critical, so all my gear fits in a small daypack, allowing me to get in, set up, shoot, and get out quickly.

While most photography captures an instant—a fraction of a second— night photography is about recording a span of time measurable in human terms. Capturing a scene takes on different meaning with the knowledge that moonlight is slowly accumulating in the camera with every tick of the watch. Minutes-long exposures record the stars spiraling around Polaris as the Earth rotates. Trees blur in the wind, and clouds are smeared

across the sky, reflecting the glow of cities beyond the horizon. People moving through the frame never appear, while planes and cars leave arcing ribbons of light. As the moon travels along its path, shadow edges become indistinct, softening the overall quality of light. Recording these deserted places with time exposures reveals their stillness, but also, the ever-changing world they inhabit.

There's minimal post-production on these images—some dodge and burn, the occasional lens-flare cleanup, perspective correction, and a few multi-exposure composites. But those are the exceptions—most of these captures are virtually untouched, straight out of the camera, with all of the scene's warts and blemishes intact.

Accessing locations can pose the biggest challenge. I've crawled into basements through muddy, greasy two-foot holes, and bicycled up and down mountains in the middle of the night on treacherous fire trails. I watched another explorer crawl up the side of a building and slink along a ledge like Spider-Man to reach a prized location. Not me, though—my ankle still aches from falling off a ten-foot-high fence six months ago. On the other hand, I was granted access from owners, caretakers, and managers for some of the locations in this book. While some explorers think half the fun is in the trespassing, I prefer permission if possible. Not having to worry about getting caught sneaking in gives me one less thing to worry about.

And there *are* plenty of other things to worry about—even the safest-seeming location is fraught with danger. Squatters, copper bandits, and partying teenagers lurk around every corner, ready to cause problems—especially on a full moon, which is my main light source for shooting exteriors. The sites are filthy and toxic: asbestos, heavy metals, and mold are everywhere. There's always a sharp piece of metal or glass poking out in the dark, ready to rip you up. And then there's the natural world: black widow spiders as big as your thumb, clouds of ravenous mosquitoes, skunks, agitated rattlesnakes—and, my personal favorite, swarms of squeaking, circling bats.

Night photography is slow and methodical work, involving long, sometimes tedious hours. I revel in the lonely quietude, but for some it can be excruciatingly boring. In the single-digit hours, it's easy to get frustrated by the smallest thing—fumbling in the dark, dropping equipment, and tripping over your tripod legs. It's especially difficult on the third late night in a row, when sleep deprivation makes your eyes feel like atomic fireballs and you start to lose your motor skills. That's when the *really* stupid mistakes happen.

Combining urban exploration with night photography is a high-risk, high-reward pursuit. There's a daredevil streak in all of us, but what keeps me coming back is the spooky and surreal atmosphere. These places are different from the regular world; they're outside the realm of normal life—especially at night when the moon is high. Night shooters are a moonstruck bunch—we're obsessed and compelled by it. Like werewolves, we're drawn to it, transformed into something else as it waxes. We're mild-mannered citizens turned lunatics with tripods—living on a twenty-eight-day cycle, itching to get out and bask in the glow. These images are the end result of that obsession. See you in the dark.

BYRON HOT SPRINGS HOTEL

Though abandoned now, this resort hotel complex near the town of Byron, lost in the dusty hills between Oakland and Stockton, California, has a long history.

Bathed in by the Bolbones Indians for centuries, the therapeutic hot springs were discovered in the 18th century by white fur trappers. The springs quickly became an important stopover on California's early trade routes.

This ornate Beaux Arts–style four-story brick hotel—the third major structure to be built at this location—opened in 1914. During the Jazz Age, the Byron Hotel golf course was popular with San Francisco socialites and Hollywood stars, including Fatty Arbuckle and Clark Gable. The San Francisco Seals baseball team even used this luxurious hotspot for its spring training, taking advantage of the mineral pools and mud baths. During the Great Depression however, the resort spiraled into decline, finally closing in 1938.

During World War II, the War Department commandeered the hotel, renaming it "Camp Tracy" and conducting secret German and Japanese POW interrogations there. More than 1,500 prisoners passed through Byron between 1942 and 1945. During the war, the base commander had the springs capped because he found the sulfuric smell offensive, and they remain sealed to this day.

In 1946, the military sold the hotel to the Greek Orthodox Church, which converted it into a monastery named Mission St. Paul. It closed a decade later in 1956.

Starting in the late '50s, the resort was sold and resold to a long list of developers who all had big plans to rejuvenate it. Every effort failed. The current owners still want to redevelop the spot as a major resort destination. In the meantime, suburban Contra Costa County sprawls closer and closer.

There are rumors that the hotel is haunted. On a shoot one full-moon night, I found a paranormal research team wandering the hallways while taking readings on handheld machines that looked like props right out of *Ghostbusters*. A medium led the parade, muttering, "I feel the presence of a military man . . ." in hushed tones.

I've spent many nights here over the last couple of years, alone and in groups, and while I find the hotel to be exceedingly creepy, I've never heard anything that couldn't be explained as wind under the eaves or birds rustling around.

And yet, on another trip, my lighting equipment kept shutting off for no apparent reason, which never happened to me before. When I dropped one of my gels and bent to pick it up, a gentle gust of wind kept blowing it a few feet out of reach . . . over and over again. The place has a haunting vibe—so the imagination can easily run wild.

Of more concern than the existence of ghosts, however, are the very real packs of hoodlum teenagers playing *A Clockwork Orange* out here. Several of the small buildings on the grounds have recently burned down, and these vandals have kicked down large sections of the walls in the kitchen/office wing. Despite the current owner's visions of restoration, the hotel will likely be reduced to rubble soon, either by developers or tweaker teenagers.

Chimney, 2007. Looking out the vent hole in the heavily damaged kitchen. To the south, waves of fog break over Tracy.

Sniper, 2007 (opposite). The burned and smashed kitchen commands the high ground above the windswept Contra Costa hills as a front blows in.

Overview, 2005. Sad and forgotten, the once stately hotel vainly tries to hide ɔm vandals behind its screen of swaying palms.

Pantry, 2007. This blown-out kitchen wall reveals the rugged concrete frame of this "fire-proof" structure.

Red Brick Dream, 2007. Lost in deep shadows, the employee's entrance at the rear of the service wing beckons, daring you to enter. This entire wall collapsed in 2007.

Barrow, 2007 (opposite). Looking south from the site of the Mead Cottage. Torched by vandals in 2005, scorched rubble is all that remains.

Lefty Loosey, 2007. Looking north out of the corrugated metal boiler shack while it ceaselessly creaks and chatters in the wind.

Twins, 2007 (right). This basement is all that remains of the original hotel, burned in 1912 and replaced by the current brick-and-concrete structure.

Sparrow in the Can, 2005. Inside one of the complex's service buildings—birds don't usually sit still for light painting.

Framed Frames, 2007 (opposite). Looking to the south through the destroyed ground-floor barbershop.

Hot Spot, 2007. The weekend before the 4th of July saw several small brushfires on the property. This one was still glowing well past midnight in the hot, gusty wind.

DESERT

Until about two hundred years ago, the deserts of the American West sustained only a small, often nomadic population. The climate is harsh, with summer temperatures soaring into the 100s. The winds can be relentless, and winter nights are bitterly cold. Water is scarce, except for the summers, when monsoon rains cause massive flash floods. These inhospitable conditions have kept most humans away throughout history.

Then in 1849, the California Gold Rush and the dawn of the American industrial age poured a tidal wave of fortune seekers into this unforgiving environment. Soon the desert territories exploded with gold, silver, and copper mining. Many of the mines played out in a few short years, and the boomtowns they created quickly slid into decline—sometimes turning into ghosts almost overnight. Even today, the region is littered with mining relics, although the vast majority of the Old West's settlements have vanished without a trace.

The advent of air-conditioning, affordable cars, and unbridled postwar optimism kick-started a new wave of Western expansion in the second half of the 20th century. By way of Route 66, the desert once again bloomed with growth.

But the 1970s brought another cycle of contraction. This was the era of the failed subdivision. Real estate speculators lost their shirts on thousand-acre, high-desert developments that were nothing more than shimmering mirages dancing in the creosote. The '70s also saw the death of the two-lane roadside town—murder by bypass—as the straight line–obsessed interstates steamrolled by, just out of reach. In only a few short years, local economies were devastated, and entire towns were snuffed out. The ruthless natural environment accelerated the downward spiral, leaving only dilapidated buildings and the skeletons of gas pumps. Hundreds of forgotten crossroads lace the American outback, each one ripe for exploration.

The entire modern Western lifestyle was built around the automobile, and the desert remains the last resting place for millions of them. Abandoned cars abound: a finned, atomic-age "spacecraft" decaying peacefully in a field twenty miles from the nearest town; a bulbous postwar hulk sitting up to its door handles in weeds behind an abandoned gas station; an unidentifiable derelict lying on its roof in a culvert, peppered with buckshot.

The desert is also strewn with automobile junkyards. On the fringes of every town you'll find at least one. Some are small mom-and-pop shops with a handful of cars; others are enormous corporate operations. The best have a couple of rows of '50s and '60s cars out back, crawling with spiders and rust. These are the owners' private collections, hidden behind a sea of sad late-model wrecks. Ask nicely, and they might let you in to pay homage.

When a junkyard is abandoned, it brings a double helping of desolation. Only a few rotten carcasses are left behind—moonbathing along shattered fence lines. Spending time with these crumbling dinosaurs, it's hard to imagine they were once someone's gleaming pride and joy.

Trailer Moonrise, 2006. The full moon crests the thunderheads as a decaying streamlined trailer sleeps through its last summer in the abandoned Route 66 junkyard at Hodge, California. All the vehicles in this junkyard, including this trailer, were removed in 2007.

Lenticular, 2007 (page 32). Closed in 1917, not much remains of the Llano Socialist Community. Fifty miles away, over the San Gabriel Mountains, the lights of Los Angeles bounce off the fast-moving winter clouds.

Two Posts, 2006. This '50s panel truck sits on its chassis, stranded alongside the nonexistent fence, at the unnamed junkyard in Hodge, California. Fifteen miles away, Barstow glows on the horizon. This junkyard was cleaned out in 2007, and this truck hauled off to another junkyard.

Four Burners, 2007. Inside another creaky building, lost someplace in the deserts of the American West.

Insurance Too, 2006 (opposite). Is there anything more ironic than an abandoned real estate office? Neglected and forsaken on a deserted road near El Mirage, California.

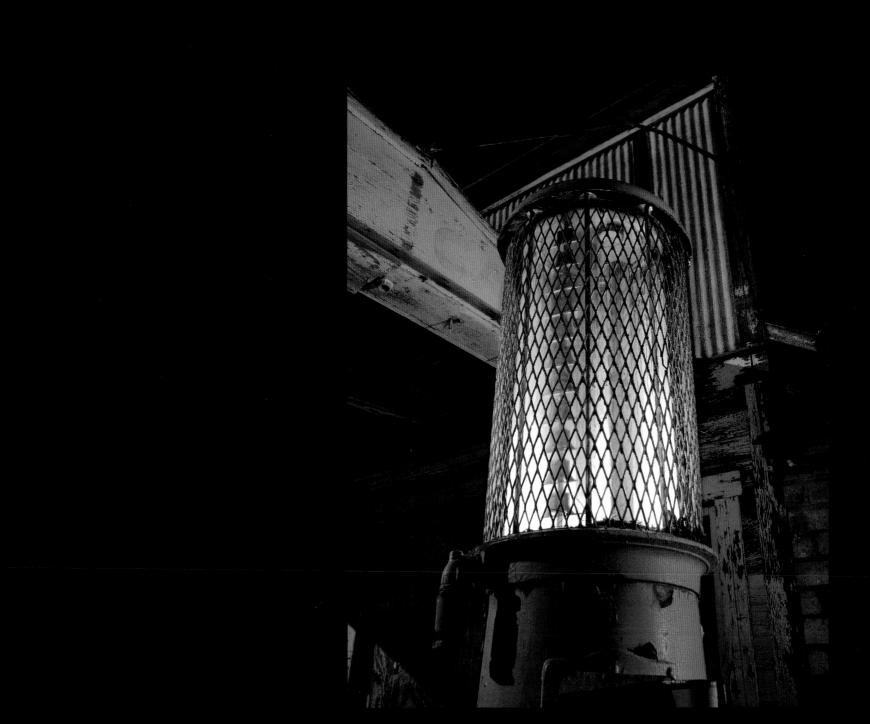

The Sofa Graveyard, 2006. A warehouse building in remote New Idria, California, mysteriously filled with dozens of moldy sofas, stacked on end.

16TH STREET TRAIN STATION

I lucked into accessing the Oakland Southern Pacific Station at the lowest ebb in its history—a rainy night in 2005. Another photographer, who had befriended the night watchman, invited me along. With a wave of his hand, the old guy gave us the run of the place. High above the platform, fast-moving storm clouds were blurred across the churning sodium-vapor-lit sky, providing an appropriately unsettled backdrop for this looming stone monster.

Unfortunately, the beautifully patinaed interior walls had recently been tagged with graffiti by the crew of the musical film *Rent* to make the location feel more "street." Damaging abandoned sites is typical for film crews, but even their abuse couldn't ruin this amazing place. Nearby street lamps cast complex shadows from the window mullions into the great-room. The enormous lobby resembled a decrepit mausoleum for titans, a forlorn ghost of the great railroad era.

Designed by Jarvis Hunt in the Beaux Arts style and completed in 1912, the 16th Street Station was the last stop on the transcontinental railroad for more than seventy years. This "end of the line" became a new beginning for tens of thousands of migrating Americans. It also connected the Interurban Electric Railway's "Big Red" trains to San Francisco via the lower deck of the Bay Bridge. During the Golden Age of the railroad, all lines pointed to 16th and Wood, the bustling transit hub of the entire East Bay.

In the first half of the 20th century, nearly every major American city boasted a similarly grand train station, but by the 1960s, the automobile had eclipsed the train as the dominant form of transportation in America. Most of the stations were closed and abandoned by the 1970s, and by the '80s, only a few had avoided the wrecking ball. Southern Pacific Railroad leased the 16th Street Station to Amtrak in 1971, and it soldiered on through the dark years, becoming dingy and frayed. To offer it some protection from developers, it was declared a city landmark in 1984, but after suffering structural damage in 1989's Loma Prieta earthquake, its doors closed for good. Now lost in the shadow of the new "MacArthur Maze" freeway interchange and disconnected from *any* train tracks, this massive stone edifice has slumbered, utterly forgotten, for almost twenty years.

There were moments in the 1990s when the crippled station seemed about to be razed, but it managed to cling to life with the help of local activists. In late 2005, a compromise was reached between local citizens and developers for "The Wood Street Project." The plan is to incorporate the 20,000-square-foot station into the redevelopment of the entire twenty-nine-acre site. The nine-block-long, mixed-use facility—including 1,500 residential units—will rejuvenate this blighted part of the city, while saving the classic historic building. As of this writing, construction of the first phase is underway.

The Caretaker, 2005. Incandescent light streams in from the night watchman's room as the outside sodium-vapor streetlights softly bathe the lobby through the ornate window mullions.

The End of the Line, 2005 (page 60). Roadbeds to nowhere stand defiantly before the storm clouds smeared over the glowing midnight skies.

Wingbacks, 2005. Dwarfed by the massive lobby, are these leftover props from a movie production, or the caretaker's impromptu break room?

Chiaroscuro, 2005 (opposite). Lit by the streetlights burning through the gallery of windows on the opposite wall, the gift shop promotes arcane technology.

Into the Abyss, 2005. The station platform stairs lead down into the open-air baggage-claim area, while the endless traffic streams by on Interstate 880.

The Blueprint Room, 2005. Deep inside this building's dark bowels is the gigantic blueprint room, packed with mostly empty flat-file drawers.

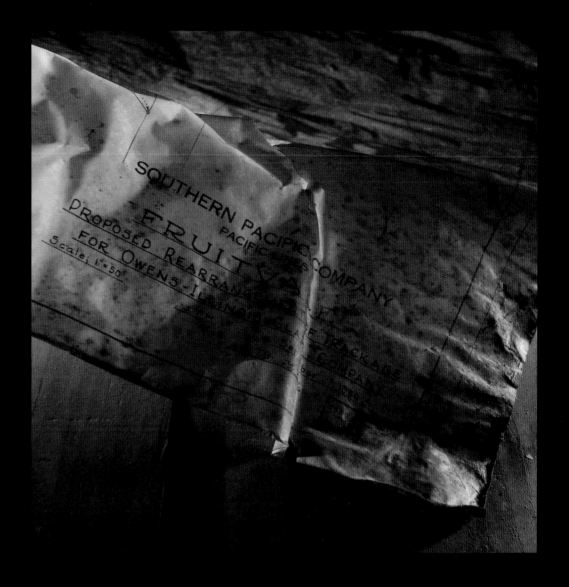

Fruitvale Plans, 2005. A moldy original vellum plan dating from 1950, found rotting on the floor of the blueprint room.

The Ladies' Room, 2005 (opposite). Water seeps into the lobby from the broken and battered women's room.

Lamp, 2005. October rains soak a broken lamppost and fence overlooking West Oakland's industrial wastelands.

DECOMMISSIONED

The mobilization of American armed forces during World War II prompted a massive surge of military base construction on the home front. City-sized training facilities capable of processing tens of thousands of draftees through boot camp were built seemingly overnight. Airfields and shipyards were erected on an epic scale to serve the machines of war.

With the close of WWII came the Cold War and the nuclear arms race. This meant more military expansion along with increasing technological sophistication. Specialized missile defense and radio interception installations soon sprang up across the nation.

Perched on the brink of Armageddon for decades, Americans were surrounded by underground missile silos, NORAD sites, and top-secret electronic surveillance bases. Hidden in plain sight, a mysterious shadow world was secluded behind miles of barbed-wire fences and M16-toting MPs.

The fall of the Berlin Wall in 1989 and subsequent collapse of the Soviet Union set off a chain reaction of American military downsizing. Over the next fifteen years the U.S. Department of Defense closed more than 350 installations deemed redundant or outdated. Many bases were immediately decommissioned, sold for development, and razed without fanfare. Others were simply abandoned, their gates left wide open. Hundreds are dangerous Superfund sites loaded with chemical toxins, unexploded ordnance, and radioactive contamination—certain to be a liability for generations to come.

You can get an overwhelming feeling of desolation on the remote rural installations. Run-down and overgrown, they look like post-apocalyptic movie sets. The feeling of melancholia and tragic waste is palpable for some urban explorers—others feel like they are slinking through a real-life video game, half-jokingly on the lookout for shambling zombies.

The sprawling subdivisions abide. Appliances and furniture have been dragged into the streets and left to rot. Winter rains can leave whole neighborhoods flooded for weeks, the standing water as smooth as glass. There are no city services to call to come clear these drains, but they wouldn't hear your voice anyway over the croaking of thousands of moonlight-crazed frogs.

Copper thieves run rampant on some bases. Destructive scavengers sledgehammering buildings to pieces, tearing out wiring and plumbing for their salvage value. Entire complexes have been gutted in short order by these criminals, leaving heaps of smashed debris and clouds of asbestos dust in their wake.

If they are isolated enough, the abandoned housing tracts are sometimes converted into tactical combat training areas by the military. Navy SEALs blast through ceilings and walls, practicing forced-entry techniques, while junk cars are placed in strategic lines of sight, flipped and crushed by tanks. These suburban battlefields complete the jarring, parallel-universe quality of the military's deserted communities.

Meanwhile, on most bases, demolition is the order of the day as bulldozers relentlessly chew through acres of empty warehouse, office, and barracks buildings. At the current breakneck pace of redevelopment, most of the closed bases will vanish completely in a few more years.

The Cube, 2007. This seven-story concrete cube once housed some of the most advanced radar equipment in the world, protecting America from missile attack. Built in 1957, this Air Force radar station was closed in 1980.

Deconsecrated, 2006 (page 76)**.** The full moon peeks through the fog, lighting one of the many boarded-up churches, at Fort Ord Army Base in Monterey, California.

The Big Man's Chair, 2007. The richly appointed top-floor corner office over-looking the shipyard dry docks and gantry cranes. This was the office of a magnate.

In the Keyhole, 2007. Shooting from the three-point line at a desolate mountaintop Air Force base, abandoned and untouched for almost thirty years.

Micro Marsh, 2007 (opposite). A marsh grows in the pool outside the gym at a long abandoned Air Force base. Mysterious nocturnal animals were splashing and rustling in the reeds during this exposure.

91

Crows Nest, 2006. A few of the hundreds of barracks and mess structures at Fort Ord Army Base, peacefully awaiting the bulldozer, under racing winter clouds. By 2010 the entire recruit housing area, constituting hundreds of acres, will be redeveloped.

Radiator Glow, 2007 (opposite). Inside the ladies' powder room of an abandoned shipyard office building.

Frog Farm, 2005. Record rainfalls flooded part of the residential section of decommissioned and abandoned Skaggs Island Naval Base, as another storm prepares to blow in.

Motorpool, 2007 (opposite). A battered gas pump festers, sitting atop a decaying fuel tank outside a prefab Air Force motor pool building.

Second-Floor Landing, 2007. The ornate 1917 Beaux Arts lobby of a shipyard office building, closed and uninhabited (except for a pack of feral cats) since 1989.

Ice-Cube Trays, 2007 (opposite). The broken symmetry of vandalized postwar light fixtures in an abandoned shipyard office lobby. These offices oversaw more than 10,000 employees working in three shifts during WWII.

Red Girder, 2006. Smashed windows top the walls at the indoor Olympic-size pool at Fort Ord, a decommissioned Army base slated for demolition.

Return All Tools, 2005 (opposite). The ghosts of missing tools in the motor pool building at Skaggs Island Naval Base, which was deemed redundant and closed in 1993.

Six Red Lights, 2007. This dingy corner office overlooks a quiet, late-night industrial neighborhood. This office block was the nerve center of the shipyards, overseeing the construction of seventy-two ships during WWII.

Danger Zone, 2007 (opposite). Inside Building 4900, a factory-like heavy industry structure at Fort Ord Army Base in Monterey, California.

Chernobyl, 2007. The smell of kerosene hangs heavy in the air inside the control room of the powerhouse at a decommissioned Air Force radar station.

Cyclops, 2007 (opposite). A decrepit truck scale found in the industrial section of Fort Ord Army Base, which was demolished in 2007.

The Cube From the Can, 2007. Originally part of the NORAD missile defense network, this derelict Air Force station has been closed for almost thirty years. This is the view from the foul-smelling men's room.

Wiring Access, 2007 (opposite). Heavy-duty underground wiring channels run from building to building at an abandoned mountaintop Air Force radar station.

Seal Hole, 2006. Navy SEALs, practicing forced-entry techniques, used shaped charges to blow neat circular holes in the reinforced concrete walls and ceiling of Building 21, at Skaggs Island Naval Base.

Drydock 4, 2004. Overlooking one of the flooded dry docks at San Francisco's Hunters Point Naval Shipyard, as a fire truck drives by, its lights blazing.

Pump House, 2004 (right). This brick pump house, operating the first dry dock on the West Coast, was built in 1867. Boarded up for decades

Air Traffic, 2004. Airliners out of San Francisco International turn west, toward the Pacific, over decommissioned Hunters Point Naval Shipyard. This crane was dismantled for scrap in 2006.

BONEYARD

El Mirage dry lake is a sleepy, windblown spot, lost in an isolated corner of Southern California's high desert. Its six-mile-long patch of smooth, hard-packed surface makes it a perfect runway. Consequently, it was used as an auxiliary airfield for nearby Victorville Air Force Base during WWII. After it was turned over for civilian use, aside from hot rodders using the lakebed for a few high-speed events each year, it has remained little used.

Today, this quiet backwater is the locale for Mark Thomson's busy Aviation Warehouse, a provider of aviation-related material for the film and TV industry. Thomson started out flying charter and camera planes in the '60s, eventually moving into buying and selling aircraft parts for film props. His business started modestly; in the early '70s he supplied a crashed airframe for the TV show *Emergency!*, and from this he forged lifelong contacts with Hollywood art directors and set designers. Before he knew it, Thomson had become the foremost supplier of aeronautical props in the business.

In 1980, Thomson bought the airport at El Mirage and moved his operation from Hawthorne in the Los Angeles metro area to the desert, where land was cheap and he could spread out. Over the years, he has amassed a tremendous stockpile of worn-out and junk aircraft, from tiny Cessnas to wide-body airliners, as well as military transports and fighters. Many of these airframes are carefully broken and smashed to simulate fiery crash scenes, their fuselages torn and painted flat black. Thomson has supplied planes and parts for more than three hundred movies, including *True Lies*, *War of the Worlds*, *Mission: Impossible*, and *Con Air*. If a movie has a plane crash in it, the airframe probably came from Aviation Warehouse.

Closed to the public, quiet and deserted, the sprawling Aviation Warehouse yard is an overwhelming sight. It's easy to get lost wandering the winding sandy trails that separate the different types of planes and parts. One way to navigate the yard is to follow the landmarks—make a left at the mountain of airliner seats, walk past the row of massive landing gear, and you'll find the Lockheed Harpoon, next to the alley of engine nacelles.

Thomson is well aware of the history and romance of his collection. The smashed and shredded debris is arranged around the twisted Joshua trees in strangely artistic piles. Thomson tries to keep it this way to help producers and art directors visualize the potential of his best pieces, but it's a constant battle to keep the yard from slipping into jumbled anarchy. He clearly loves what he's doing, creating a space that is part junkyard, part prop-house, and part museum.

Poking through this boneyard at night is an unforgettable experience. Thick with atmosphere, it's a Disneyland for urban explorers and junk geeks. Most people view airliners as permanent, a constant in their lives. They prefer not to envision aircraft wearing out, but the reality is that they will eventually reach a point where they are destined for the scrap heap, just like cars or refrigerators. It's an unsettling experience to see these icons of everyday technology smashed and broken, disappearing into the sand—an eerie reminder that time is short, and *nothing* is permanent.

Clipped and Headless, 2006. A brutalized Delta 727 fuselage flopped on its belly in the sand, a multiple amputee.

Sahara, 2006 (page 116). Lying on its belly in the dunes, this twin-tailed Lockheed Harpoon took decades to acquire its sandblasted patina.

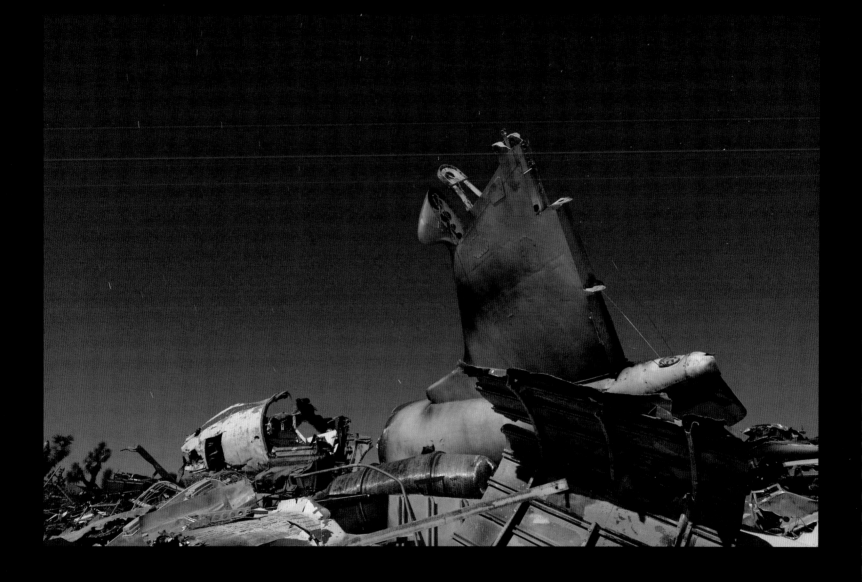

Tail, 2006. Shattered and smashed piles of exotic debris stretch to the horizon. Aviation Warehouse is a fantasyland for junkyard geeks.

The Finger of Doom, 2006 (opposite). Some of the heavy equipment used to break junk airliners into bite-size chunks for the smelter.

Big Gear, 2007. The main landing gear of a wide-body airliner towers over the yard.

Crow's Nest, 2006 (opposite). This spiral staircase to the first-class lounge, sectioned out of a 747, would be a perfect addition to any clubhouse.

Joshua Says Go!, 2006. A '40s-vintage Lockheed Harpoon gets launch instructions from a Joshua tree.

Coated, 2006 (opposite). Piles of old-school analog gauges gather dust in the huge parts shed.

Apocalypse Now, 2006. A Vietnam-era Huey awaits a call to duty that will never come, below an incoming aircraft, streaking east. Don't forget to sit on your helmet.

Crash Simulation, 2006. Shattered fuselage pieces creak and sway in the desert wind.

Celestial Navigation, 2006. The front fuselage section of a Douglas DC-4, rolled on its side. The dome was used to navigate by the stars.

Flight Engineer, 2007 (opposite). The cockpit of a KC-97 Stratotanker collects dust, untouched for decades

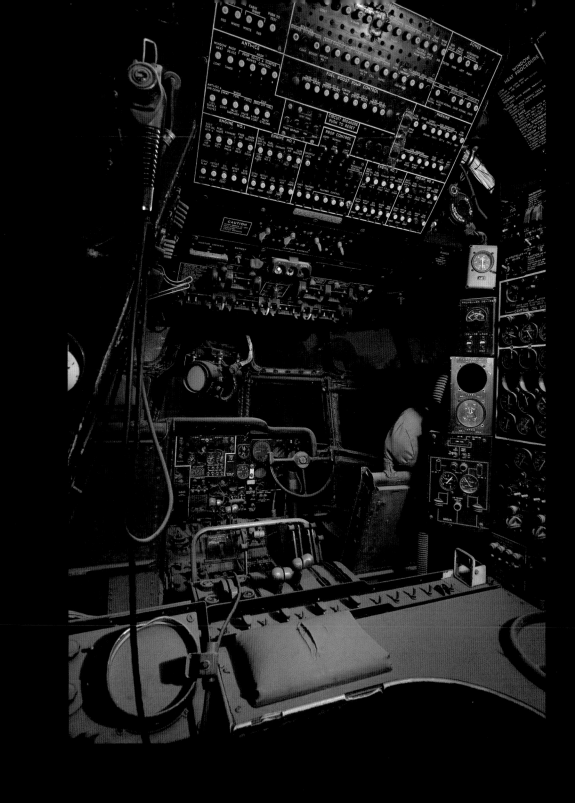

Dinosaur, 2006. Carefully broken and painted flat black to simulate a fiery crash, this 707 fuselage awaits its next movie role.

EST, 2007 (opposite). The main cabin door, sectioned out of a Northwest Airlines DC 10, sits in the dunes under heavy skies.

Breathe Normally, 2006. The oxygen masks are deployed, along with the entire ceiling, in a decapitated airliner.

Aloha From the Land of Jets and Joshuas, 2006 (right). Like a tossed aside toy, a smashed and broken Hawaiian Airlines 737 fuselage lays on its side, ready for recycling.

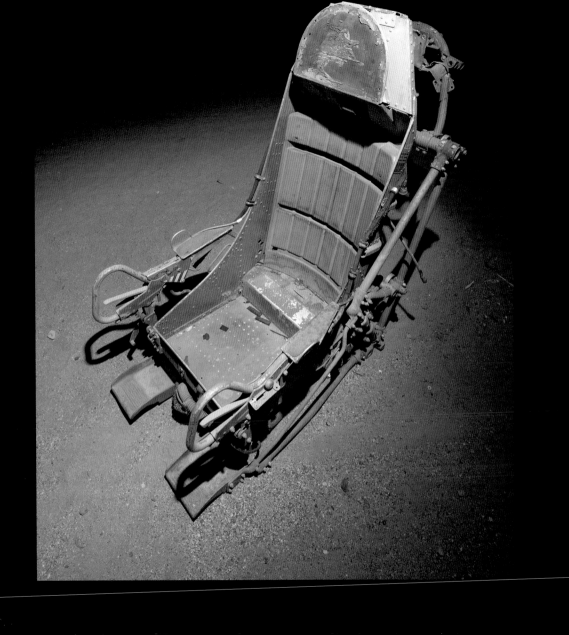

PRA, 2006. A pair of movie-prop aircraft depicting two different fates slumber side by side.

Eject!, 2006 (opposite). An ejection seat from a '50s-era fighter jet sits in the sand. It was so heavy I could barely move it.

139

Yard Ornaments, 2006. Jumbo jet nacelle and Joshua tree, basking in the moon.

Do I know you? If so, then you had something to do with the genesis of this book. The list of names is just too long to even consider. Thanks to everyone who shapes my perception, making me who I am, making my photography what it is.

Several of these sites would have been impossible to shoot this way without the access granted by Patricia McFadden, Ray Meyer at Antelope Valley Auto Wreckers, Mark Thomson of Aviation Warehouse, and the guy at that place who doesn't want to be named. Thanks for "getting it" instantly, and turning me loose.

I was made aware of many of these locations by photographers Jon Haeber, Riki Feldman, Shadow Of Light Project, Andy Frazer, Steve Anderson, Shane Donaghy, Joe Reifer, Steve Walsh, Basim Jaber, and Lane Hartwell. Thanks for going shooting; was that fun or what?

And a low-angled wash of red-gelled flashlight to *all* the UE night photographers out there. There sure are a lot more of you now, and nothing makes me happier. Turn off those goofy headlamps and let the fool moon be your guide.

Special nods go to Steve Harper, Tim Baskerville, Lance Keimig, and especially my brother Tom—the Mount Rushmore of West Coast night photography. Larrie Thomson, too, dude, you rawk. My work would have never made it out of the '90s without all of your work and encouragement. You guys helped to keep night photography alive through it's darkest days.

The writing in this book was a *real* mess until Jeff Breitenstein, Tom Moore, and Joe Reifer got a hold of it. Thanks for your clear thoughts, insanely logical arguments, and polysyllabic slapitude. You guys made it fun and easy.

Thanks also to the editorial and design crew at Chronicle Books for handling the short gestation and difficult birth of this baby without batting an eye: Alan Rapp, Bridget Watson Payne, Doug Ogan, Jay Peter Salvas, River Jukes-Hudson, Matthew Boyd, and Tera Killip.

Sweem, thanks for the use of the hall!

This book is the product of an obsession. All my love goes to my wife, Jooolie, who gives me the freedom to obsess.

ACKNOWLEDGMENTS